BIRDS

Devised and written by Jen Green

CONTENTS

Designed by Nicola Chapman and Suzanne Perkins

Photographs by Kim Taylor

Illustrations by Edwina Hannam, Sarah John and Mainline Design

zigzag

WHAT ARE BIRDS?

There are more birds on Earth than any other kind of warm-blooded animal. The key to their success is the ability to fly, which allows them to escape from danger and to travel far in search of food. Birds are the only animals with feathers. They have beaks, instead of jaws with teeth, and scaly legs and feet. All birds lay eggs. There are about 8,600 different kinds, or species, of birds in the world. Scientists divide them into 27 groups called orders, and the orders into 155 different families.

The Purple Glossy-Starling comes from North Africa.

Great White Pelicans are fish-eating birds of seas and lakes.

WHERE BIRDS ARE FOUND

Birds live all over the world, in different *habitats*, or homes, from baking deserts to frozen icecaps, and from jungles to the open seas. Almost two-thirds of all bird species live in the world's rainforests. Because birds are warm-blooded they are able to keep their body temperature even, so they can stay active even in very hot or very cold weather.

Owls are birds of woods and fields. Most kinds sleep by day and are active at night.

The first bird-like creature known to science is the Archaeopteryx, which lived about 150 million years ago. Fossils show that Archaeopteryx was about the same size as a gull, with sharp teeth, feathered wings and a long tail. It was not a strong flier but could glide down from a height. Claws on the front of each wing may have helped it to climb trees to launch itself into the air.

LARGEST AND SMALLEST

Birds vary greatly in color and size. The largest bird is the African Ostrich, which can grow up to 9 ft tall. The smallest is the Bee Hummingbird from Cuba, just over 2 ins long. The Wandering Albatross, which spends most of its life flying over the southern oceans, has the greatest wingspan, 11 ft, and is also one of the world's heaviest flying birds.

African Ostrich

Wandering Albatross

Bee Hummingbird

3

PARTS OF A BIRD

A bird's whole body is designed for flight. Although they vary in size, most flying birds share a similar body shape, so that air can pass freely around the bird's body without slowing down its speed in flight. This is called a *streamlined* shape.

The shape of some parts of the body varies in different families of birds. For example, the bill, neck and legs of a Great Blue Heron are longer than those of the Jackdaw. Looking at the shape of the wings and tail, and the length of the neck and legs, can help you to identify birds. It can also tell you about their way of life.

PLUMAGE

The color of a bird's *plumage* (feathers) is important for its survival. It allows the bird to recognize others of its species. It may help the bird to blend in with its surroundings, to attract a mate, or warn away a rival.

A bird's brain is small but birds are naturally able to do many things. This ability is called *instinct*. Some species, such as this Jackdaw, also show intelligent behavior.

Wing

Rump

Tail

Breast

Throat

Belly

Claw

Nape

Crown

Nostril

Beak or bill

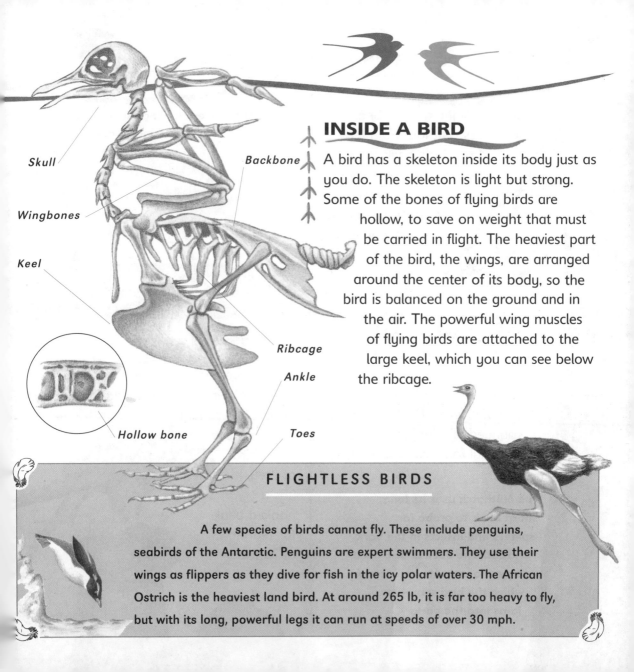

Skull

Wingbones

Keel

Backbone

Ribcage

Ankle

Toes

Hollow bone

INSIDE A BIRD

A bird has a skeleton inside its body just as you do. The skeleton is light but strong. Some of the bones of flying birds are hollow, to save on weight that must be carried in flight. The heaviest part of the bird, the wings, are arranged around the center of its body, so the bird is balanced on the ground and in the air. The powerful wing muscles of flying birds are attached to the large keel, which you can see below the ribcage.

FLIGHTLESS BIRDS

A few species of birds cannot fly. These include penguins, seabirds of the Antarctic. Penguins are expert swimmers. They use their wings as flippers as they dive for fish in the icy polar waters. The African Ostrich is the heaviest land bird. At around 265 lb, it is far too heavy to fly, but with its long, powerful legs it can run at speeds of over 30 mph.

BEAKS AND FEET

Tough and light, a bird's beak has many uses. Without front legs, a bird needs its beak to catch, prepare and hold its food. The beak is also used for *preening*, cleaning the feathers, and when making nests. You may be able to guess what a bird eats and where it finds its food from the shape of its bill. Some small garden birds, such as finches, have short, cone-shaped beaks for breaking open seeds. Ducks have flat, rounded bills for straining plant and animal food from fresh water.

The Nuthatch uses its long, sharp beak to probe for spiders and insects in the bark of trees. The beak is also used to peck open nuts and acorns which the bird sometimes jams into the bark.

The Lesser Flamingo feeds with its head held upside-down in shallow water. Its beak is used to sieve shrimps and other food from the water.

HUNTER'S BEAK

Birds of prey are those that hunt and feed on other animals (their *prey*). This Eurasian Kestrel has caught a mouse. Like other birds of prey, it has a hooked beak for tearing at its food.

FEET

A bird's feet are also designed to suit the place where it lives and its way of life. Feet are used for preening, swimming, climbing, perching and holding food as well as for hopping, walking or running. The Fish Eagles and Osprey are birds of prey with strong, hooked claws for seizing and carrying away slippery fish. The webbed feet of ducks and geese act as paddles to push them through the water.

With their broad bodies and webbed feet, these ducklings are well suited to a life on water.

PERCHING

Garden birds such as this Eurasian Bullfinch spend much of their lives perched on branches. They have three toes pointing forwards and one pointing backwards. These allow the bird's feet to lock around the branch, so it does not fall even when resting.

A Blue and Yellow Macaw holds a walnut in its claw while cracking open the shell with its strong, hooked beak.

FINDING FOOD

Seeds, grains, worms, beetles, fish and mice are all the food of different kinds of birds. Some birds can only eat one particular sort of food, while others have a varied diet. A bird's senses are well suited to search for its particular food.

The most important senses for most birds are sound and especially sight. A bird of prey, such as the Eurasian Kestrel, has keen eyesight, up to five times more powerful than a human. Hovering in the wind, they can spot a mouse in the grass up to a thousand yards. below, and swoop down steeply to catch it in their claws.

THE PERFECT HUNTER

Some birds of prey such as owls are *nocturnal*, which means they sleep by day and hunt at night. This Barn Owl's senses are perfect for night-hunting. Its large eyes allow it to see small prey animals even in dim light. Its excellent hearing can pick up the tiny squeaks and rustles of its victim.

A Barn Owl swoops down silently on its prey.

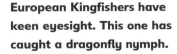

European Kingfishers have keen eyesight. This one has caught a dragonfly nymph.

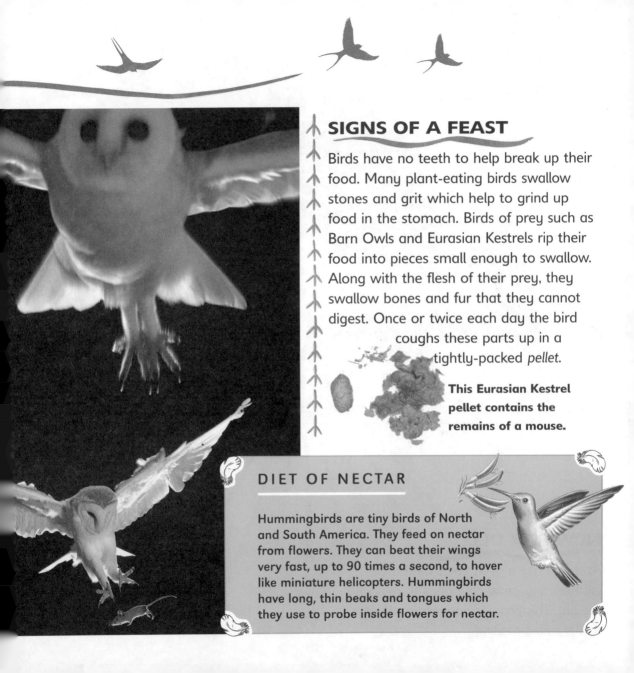

SIGNS OF A FEAST

Birds have no teeth to help break up their food. Many plant-eating birds swallow stones and grit which help to grind up food in the stomach. Birds of prey such as Barn Owls and Eurasian Kestrels rip their food into pieces small enough to swallow. Along with the flesh of their prey, they swallow bones and fur that they cannot digest. Once or twice each day the bird coughs these parts up in a tightly-packed *pellet*.

This Eurasian Kestrel pellet contains the remains of a mouse.

DIET OF NECTAR

Hummingbirds are tiny birds of North and South America. They feed on nectar from flowers. They can beat their wings very fast, up to 90 times a second, to hover like miniature helicopters. Hummingbirds have long, thin beaks and tongues which they use to probe inside flowers for nectar.

FEATHERS

Contour feather

Wing flight feather

A Coal Tit carrying a peanut.

Tail flight feather

Feathers allow a bird to fly, and also keep it dry and warm. Feathers are made of a light, strong material called keratin, which is also found in your hair and nails.

There are three main types of feathers. *Contour feathers* cover the bird's body and protect it. *Flight feathers*, found on the wings and tail, are stronger and longer than contour feathers. They are used for flying, steering and braking. *Down feathers* are found beneath the contour feathers. Soft and fluffy, they trap a layer of air next to the bird's body to keep it warm.

NEW FOR OLD

At least once a year, birds shed their feathers and grow new ones to replace the old. This process happens gradually and is called *molting*.

Down feathers   Contour feather   Flight feather

TAKING CARE OF FEATHERS

As the closeup on the right shows, a feather is made up of hundreds of tiny strands called barbs, which hook together like teeth in a zip fastener to give a smooth surface. In the course of daily life, a bird's feathers may split, and the barbs become "unzipped." Feathers are kept in good condition by *preening*. The bird draws each feather through its beak, cleaning it and gently nibbling the barbs back into position.

A Great Cormorant preens its feathers.

MATCHING COLORS

The plumage of many birds is colored to match their surroundings. This is called *camouflage*. It allows the bird to blend into the background, keeping it safe from enemies, or allowing it to hunt for prey. The plumage of some birds changes color with the seasons. The Rock Ptarmigan has brown feathers in summer, to blend in with the grasslands where it lives. In winter its plumage turns white, to match the snow.

FLYING

Gravity is the force which makes a ball you toss in the air fall back to Earth. Anything that flies must overcome this force. Birds' wings have a special shape that helps them to overcome gravity. When a bird's wing flaps up, the outer feathers open to let the air pass through. As the wing flaps down again, the feathers close to trap the air. The wing pushes against the air, sending the bird upwards and forwards.

TAKE-OFF AND LANDING

Extra effort is needed for take-off, to launch the bird into the air. Small, light birds such as European Robins (left) leap into the air, and are away with a beat of their wings. Some larger, heavier birds such as owls may drop from a high perch and flap their wings as they dive. Others, such as swans, run to gather speed before take-off. When landing, a bird must slow down as much as possible to avoid crashing. It fans out the wing and tail feathers to brake its speed, and then drops lightly to its feet.

At take-off the wing feathers are spread out. The wings beat down strongly to lift the bird.

SPEED LIMITS

Garden birds such as House Sparrows fly at about 18 mph. Barn Swallows and Common Swifts are fast-flying small birds. Their curved wings and forked tails allow them to turn and dive in the air to catch flying insects. Common Swifts fly at 25 mph.

Geese cruise along at 34 mph, and can keep up this pace for many hours. The Eider Duck is a sea duck with powerful wings for coping with winds at sea. It flies at a speed of 47 mph. The Peregrine Falcon can make a very fast power dive, pouncing on its prey at speeds of up to 112 mph.

Peregrine Falcon

A Little Owl spreads wing and tail feathers to slow down before landing.

FLIGHT PATTERNS

Different types of birds have different ways of flying, and this can help to identify them. Some small birds, such as finches, flap their wings for several beats, then fold them tight against their bodies to make a streamlined shape. So they dip and rise in flight. In contrast, ducks and geese flap their wings constantly, and have a more level flight.

Larger birds, such as the Common Buzzard, circle upwards in warm, rising air currents called thermals. By flying into the wind and flapping its wings quickly, the Eurasian Kestrel can hover above the ground, looking down in search of prey.

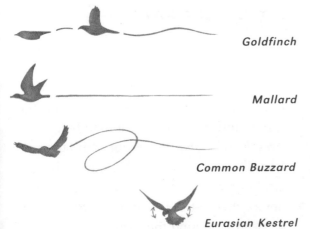

Goldfinch

Mallard

Common Buzzard

Eurasian Kestrel

MIGRATION

Many species of birds use their flying skills to travel on long journeys, to avoid the cold of winter and to go where there is plenty of food. These journeys, which occur regularly each year, are called *migrations*. Many migrating birds cover distances that are truly amazing, flying thousands of miles across continents and oceans, and then returning to the place they set out from later as the weather improves. In Europe almost half of all bird species migrate.

Each year in the fall, Brant Geese fly south from Siberia to Europe, to avoid the freezing winter. The younger birds follow the bird in front and learn the route. A group of flying geese is called a *skein*.

GETTING READY

Migrations are long, hard journeys. Many birds will die on the way, from hunger or exhaustion. Many birds do not feed while they are traveling. So they prepare for the trip by fattening up before they leave. American Golden-Plover (above) fly south from North America to Argentina. They eat large quantities of insects and shellfish before they set out, putting on fat that will be used up during the flight.

14

FINDING THE WAY

Migrating birds traveling thousands of miles find their way with amazing skill. Some learn the route by flying with their parents but many, such as the Common Cuckoo, know it by instinct. They find the way by spotting landmarks such as rivers, seas or mountain ranges, and by using sound and smell. Some birds, such as homing pigeons, use the Sun, Moon and stars to guide them and can even sense the Earth's magnetic field.

Pigeons are very skilled at finding their way.

BIRD VOICES

Simple calls often act as a warning for other birds. A Rook caws loudly to warn other members of its flock of danger.

Birds communicate with one another using a variety of calls and songs. Simple notes called *contact calls* are used to keep in touch with other birds in the same flock. Migrating geese honk to the others flying with them to help the group stay together. Contact calls are also used by birds to identify their mate or chicks. In Antarctica, penguin parents find their chicks among thousands of babies by recognizing the particular cry of their own chick.

A FAMILIAR CRY

The Northern Gannet nests in a *colony*, a large group of birds. A Northern Gannet returning to the nest (above) must find its mate among thousands of similar birds. The two birds call and can recognize one another despite a great din of similar cries.

LEARNING AN ACCENT

Birds of the same species sing the same basic song. The song is partly instinctive, a skill the bird is born with. It is also learned from its parents and others of its kind while it is growing up. In some species of bird, the basic song may vary, depending on where the bird lives. Studies on Chaffinches living in neighboring valleys showed that the song varied from valley to valley. The birds had picked up a local "accent" as they grew up.

KEEP AWAY

Many birds can produce the more complicated series of notes we call a song. Birdsong is used to establish a bird's *territory*, the patch of land where it lives and feeds. The Common Nightingale is famous for its night-time singing. It also sings during the day, to warn other birds away from the woodland bushes where it hunts for insects. Birds such as Common Nightingales also sing to attract a mate. A male Willow Warbler sings loudly to attract a female into his territory.

The beautiful melody of the Song Thrush is territorial, to warn other birds away.

FINDING A MATE

For a species to survive, a bird must find a mate to breed with and raise young. It is usually the male birds who court (try to attract) the females, with colorful feathers and special actions, called *displays*. Most females have dull colors, so they are camouflaged when sitting on the nest.

The male Indian Peafowl is a spectacular bird. Each of his tail feathers has a beautiful "eye." He spreads his tail feathers wide, and quivers them to impress females. The male Frigatebird has a red pouch on his throat. During the breeding time he attracts a mate by inflating the pouch so that it swells up like a red balloon.

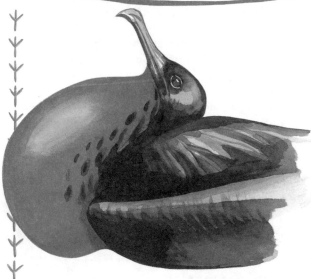

A Magnificent Frigatebird inflates his pouch.

SHOW OFF

Some birds perform a more complicated series of actions to attract a mate. When courting a female, the male European Robin (left) brings her a gift of worms to show that he is a good hunter who will be able to provide food for the young. Other birds put on displays of singing or dancing. Great-crested Grebes perform four separate dances over several weeks before they choose a mate and rear a family.

PARTNERS FOR LIFE?

Some birds, such as Mute Swans and Golden Eagles, pair and stay together for life. Others find a mate each year and stay together for the breeding season only. Species of heron and finches share the tasks of building the nest and feeding the chicks. In some bird species, the male birds mate with two or three partners in one year. The females are sometimes left to build the nest and raise the young alone.

Northern Gannet couples pair for life.

DANCING GROUND

Some kinds of male birds gather at a special communal display ground, called a *lek*, to perform their courtship dances. North American Sage Grouse males gather at the lek at dawn, and defend the best positions against rival males. The strongest birds gain ground in the center. When the females arrive, the males go into a frenzy of spectacular dancing. The females watch, sometimes weaving between the males. The females usually choose a male that has a position in the center of the lek.

BUILDING A NEST

Most birds build nests, to provide a warm, safe place for their eggs to hatch and for the chicks to grow. Birds use many different materials to make their nests. Twigs and leaves, mud, moss, grass and feathers are common materials, but wool and animal hair, string, paper and even wire and metal are sometimes used.

House Martins and Barn Swallows (below) nest on ledges and under the eaves of houses. They collect mud and mix it with their saliva to form a paste which is pushed into place. The mud sets hard to make a secure home for the young.

The Chaffinch's nest (left) is lined with soft feathers and hair, and the Eurasian Blackbird's (below) with mud and leaves.

MAKING A HOME

Once a bird has chosen a safe site for the nest, it makes hundreds of trips to collect the materials it needs for building. When these are roughly in place, the nest is worked into a cup shape. The bird turns round and round in the center of its nest, pressing down on the materials until the hollow cup is formed.

UNUSUAL NESTS

Nests come in different shapes and sizes, from the great platforms of sticks built by eagles to the tiny nests of hummingbirds. The nests of African Village Weavers are perhaps the most elaborate. Using beak and feet together, the Weavers are able to tie knots in grass. They begin a nest by knotting a loop of grass to the branch of a tree, as shown above. More grass-stems are added to form a ball-shaped nest. Some kinds of Village Weavers add a cone-shaped entrance, designed to keep out snakes.

BIRDS' NEST SOUP

In China and Singapore, the nests of Edible-nest Swiftlets are used to make birds' nest soup, which is considered a delicious food. The nests, made of the birds' saliva, are built high up on the walls of caves on the islands of Indonesia. Nest gatherers use vines as ropes and bamboo poles as ladders to reach the nests. Two nests are needed to make each bowl of soup. The taste is so highly prized that some colonies of Edible-nest Swiftlets have been in danger of becoming extinct - dying out altogether.

The nest of the Long-tailed Tit is a delicate ball of cobwebs, lichen and feathers.

EGGS AND YOUNG

Once the nest is built, the female lays her eggs. Some small garden birds such as tits lay up to a dozen eggs. Many seabirds, such as penguins and albatrosses, lay only one. The eggs are often colored to match their surroundings, so that they are well hidden. The parent bird, usually the female, sits on the eggs to keep them warm.

Inside the shell, the young bird develops, supplied with air and food. Tits' eggs take about two weeks to hatch, albatross eggs take nearly three months. Some young birds, like the Japanese Quail shown below, are well-developed at birth. Others, like the Eurasian Blackbird nestlings shown right, are bald, blind and helpless.

Young Eurasian Blackbirds beg for earthworms from their mother, gaping their mouths wide and cheeping.

Inside this egg a Japanese Quail chick is about to hatch.

The chick uses the hard egg tooth on its beak to cut through the shell.

The newly hatched chick emerges from the shell.

Young European
House
sparrow.

GROWING UP

Newly hatched birds are weak, and few can feed themselves. Many parent birds are kept busy all day bringing food to the nest. The chicks grow fast. Some become independent quickly, others take longer. The Wandering Albatross chick will be fed by its parents for up to a year. Yet after only two weeks, the Eurasian Blackbird nestlings have grown their feathers and are ready to make their first flight.

One hour old, the chick can sit up. Its feathers are waxy from the egg.

After twelve hours, the feathers are dry and fluffy.

INDEX

CREDITS

UK consultant: Ivan Nethercoat, Royal Society for Protection of Birds
Additional US research: Dr Paul Green, Director of Conservation and Education, American Birding Association

Young birders who want further information should contact Paul Green, ABA, PO Box 6599, Colorado Springs, CO 80904-6599, email paulgrn @ aba.org

This edition published in 1998 by Zigzag Publishing, a division of Quadrillion Publishing Ltd., Godalming Business Centre, Surrey GU7 1XW, Great Britain.

Distributed in the US by Smithmark Publishers, a division of US Media Holdings, Inc., 16 East 32nd Street, New York, NY 10016

ISBN 0-7651-0696-5

Printed in China
8535